GOLDSTONE RECANTS

GOLDSTONE RECANTS
*Richard Goldstone Renews Israel's
License to Kill*

Norman G. Finkelstein

O/R

OR BOOKS
NEW YORK

© 2011 Norman G. Finkelstein

Published by OR Books, New York and London.

Visit our website at www.orbooks.com.

First printing 2011

All rights reserved. No part of this book may be reproduced or transmitted in any form or by any means, electronic or mechanical, including photocopy, recording, or any information storage retrieval system, without permission in writing from the publisher, except brief passages for review purposes.

Library of Congress Cataloging in Publication Data:
A catalog record for this book is available from the Library of Congress

British Library Cataloging in Publication Data:
A catalog record for this book is available from the British Library

Paperback ISBN 978-1-935928-48-5
E-book ISBN 978-1-935928-47-8

Typeset by Wordstop

Printed by BookMobile, USA, and CPI, UK

10 9 8 7 6 5 4 3 2 1

Sections of this pamphlet have been reproduced from Norman G. Finkelstein's *"This Time We Went Too Far": Truth and Consequences of the Gaza Invasion,* now published in a revised and expanded paperback by OR Books. For more information please go to www.orbooks.com.

The author wishes to thank Maren Hackmann for her assistance in preparing this pamphlet.

ON 1 APRIL 2011, in the pages of the *Washington Post*, Richard Goldstone dropped a bombshell.

He effectively disowned the massive evidence assembled in the report carrying his name that Israel had committed multiple war crimes and possible crimes against humanity in Gaza during its 2008-9 invasion.

Israel was jubilant. "Everything that we said proved to be true," Prime Minister Benjamin Netanyahu crowed. "We always said that the IDF [Israel Defense Forces] is a moral army that acted according to international law," Defense Minister Ehud Barak declared. "We had no doubt that the truth would come out eventually," Foreign Minister Avigdor Lieberman proclaimed.

The Obama administration used the occasion of Goldstone's recantation to affirm that Israel had not "engaged in any war crimes" during the Gaza assault while the U.S. Senate unanimously called on the United Nations to "rescind" the Goldstone Report.

Some commentators have endeavored to prove by parsing his words that Goldstone did not actually recant. While there are grounds for making this argument on a technical basis, such a rhetorical strategy will not wash.

Goldstone is a distinguished jurist. He knows how to use precise language. If he did not want to sever his connection with the Report he could simply have said "I am not recanting my original report by which I still stand." He must have known exactly how his words would be spun and it is this fallout—not his parsed words—that we must now confront.

Goldstone has done terrible damage to the cause of truth and justice and the rule of law. He has poisoned Jewish-Palestinian relations, undermined the courageous work of Israeli dissenters and—most unforgivably—increased the risk of another merciless IDF assault.

There has been much speculation on why Goldstone recanted. Was he blackmailed? Did he finally succumb to the relentless hate campaign directed against him? Did he decide to put his tribe ahead of truth?

What can be said with certainty, and what I will demonstrate below, is that *Goldstone did not change his mind because the facts compelled him to reconsider his original findings.*

IN APRIL 2009 the president of the United Nations Human Rights Council appointed a "Fact-Finding Mission" to "investigate all violations of international human rights law and international humanitarian law that might have been committed at any time in the context of the military operations that were conducted in Gaza during the period from 27 December 2008 and 18 January 2009, whether before, during or after."

Richard Goldstone, former judge of the Constitutional Court of South Africa and former Prosecutor of the International Criminal Tribunals for the former Yugoslavia and Rwanda, was named head of the Mission.

The Mission's original mandate was to scrutinize only Israeli violations of human rights during the assault on Gaza, but Goldstone made his acceptance of the job conditional on broadening the mandate to include violations on all sides. The council president invited Goldstone to write the mandate himself, which Goldstone did and which the president then accepted. "It was very difficult to refuse . . . a mandate that I'd written for myself," Goldstone later observed.

Nonetheless Israel did not cooperate with the Mission on the grounds of its alleged bias.

In September 2009 the long-awaited report of the Goldstone Mission was released. It was a searing indictment not just of the Gaza invasion but also of the ongoing Israeli occupation.

The Goldstone Report found that much of the death and destruction Israel inflicted on the civilian population and infrastructure of Gaza was premeditated. The assault was said to be anchored in a military doctrine that "views disproportionate destruction and creating maximum disruption in the lives of many people as a legitimate means to achieve military and political goals." The "disproportionate destruction and violence against civilians" were said to be part of a "deliberate policy," as were the "humiliation and dehumanization of the Palestinian population."

Although Israel justified the attack on grounds of self-defense against Hamas rocket attacks, the Goldstone Report pointed to a different motive. The invasion was "aimed at punishing the Gaza population for its resilience and for its apparent support for Hamas, and possibly with the intent of forcing a change in such support."

The Report concluded that the Israeli assault on Gaza constituted "a deliberately disproportionate attack designed to punish, humiliate and terrorize a civilian population."

It ticked off a lengthy list of war crimes that Israel committed such as "willful killing, torture or inhuman treatment," "willfully causing great suffering or serious injury to body or health," "extensive destruction of property, not justified by military necessity and carried out unlawfully and wantonly," and "use of human shields."

It further found that Israeli actions that "deprive Palestinians in the Gaza Strip of their means of sustenance, employment, housing and water, that deny their freedom of movement and their right to leave and enter their own country, that limit their access to courts of law and effective remedies . . . might justify a competent court finding that crimes against humanity have been committed."

The Goldstone Report pinned primary culpability for these criminal offenses on Israel's political and military elites: "The systematic and deliberate nature of the activities . . . leave the Mission in no doubt that responsibility lies in the first place with those who designed, planned, ordered and oversaw the operations."

It also found that the fatalities, property damage, and psychological trauma resulting from Hamas's "indiscriminate" and "deliberate" rocket attacks on Israel's civilian population constituted "war crimes and may amount to crimes against humanity."

Because the Goldstone Mission (like human rights organizations) devoted a much smaller fraction of its findings to Hamas rocket attacks, critics accused it of bias. The accusation was valid, but its weight ran in the opposite direction. If one considers that the ratio of Palestinian to Israeli deaths stood at more than 100:1 and of dwellings ravaged at more than 6000:1, then the proportion of the Goldstone Report given over to death and destruction caused by

Hamas in Israel was much greater than the objective data would have warranted.

THE ISRAELI REACTION to the Goldstone Report came fast and furious. Apart from a few honorable exceptions such as *Haaretz* columnist Gideon Levy, it was subjected for months to a torrent of relentless abuse across the Israeli political spectrum and at all levels of society.

Israeli President Shimon Peres ridiculed the Goldstone Report as a "mockery of history," and Goldstone himself as a "small man, devoid of any sense of justice, a technocrat with no real understanding of jurisprudence." Prime Minister Benjamin Netanyahu purported that the Report was "a kangaroo court against Israel," and Defense Minister Ehud Barak inveighed that it was "a lie, distorted, biased and supports terror."

Former Foreign Minister Tzipi Livni declared that the Goldstone Report was "born in sin," while current Foreign Minister Avigdor Lieberman declared that it had "no legal, factual or moral value," and current Deputy Foreign Minister Danny Ayalon warned that it "provides legitimacy to terrorism" and risks "turning international law into a circus."

Former Israeli ambassador to the U.N. Dan Gillerman ripped the Report for "blatant, one-sided, anti-Israel lies," and former Israeli ambassador to the U.N. Dore Gold deemed it "one of the most potent weapons in the arsenal of international terrorist organizations."

Michael Oren, the current Israeli ambassador to the United States, intoned in the *Boston Globe* that the Goldstone Report "must be rebuffed by all those who care about peace"; alleged in an address to the American Jewish Committee that Hezbollah was one of the Report's prime beneficiaries; and reckoned in the *New Republic* that the Report was even worse than "Ahmadinejad and the Holocaust deniers."

Former IDF Chief of Staff Gabi Ashkenazi dismissed the Goldstone Report as "biased and unbalanced," while IDF senior legal advisor Avichai Mendelblit derided it as "biased, astonishingly extreme, lack[ing] any basis in reality."

The *Jerusalem Post* editorialized that the Goldstone Report was "a feat of cynical superficiality" and was "born in bias and matured into a full-fledged miscarriage of justice." Former *Haaretz* editor-in-chief David Landau lamented that the Report's "fundamental premise, that the Israelis went after civilians," eliminated any possibility of "honest debate." Settler movement leader Israel Harel deemed the Report "destructive, toxic" and misdirected "against precisely that country which protects human and military ethics more than the world has ever seen."

BACK IN THE U.S. the usual suspects rose (or sunk) to the occasion of smearing the message and the messenger. In a posting on *Commentary*'s website Max Boot dismissed the Goldstone Report as a "risible series of findings," and former U.S. ambassador to the United Nations John Bolton opined in the *Wall Street Journal* that "the logical response to this debacle is to withdraw from and defund" the Human Rights Council.

Elie Wiesel condemned the Goldstone Report as not only "a crime against the Jewish people" but also "unnecessary," ostensibly because "I can't believe that Israeli soldiers murdered people or shot children. It just can't be."

Harvard's Alan M. Dershowitz alleged that the Goldstone Report "is so filled with lies, distortions and blood libels that it could have been drafted by Hamas extremists"; that it recalled the "Protocols of the Elders of Zion" and was "biased and bigoted"; that "every serious student of human rights should be appalled at this anti-human rights and highly politicized report"; and that Goldstone was "a traitor to the Jewish people," an "evil, evil man" and—he said on Israeli television—on a par with Auschwitz "Angel of Death" Josef Mengele.

The "essence" and "central conclusion" of the Goldstone Report, according to Dershowitz, was that Israel had a "carefully planned and executed policy of deliberately targeting innocent civilians for mass murder"; that Israel's "real purpose" was "to target innocent Palestinian civilians—children, women and the elderly—for death."

In fact Dershowitz conjured a straw man: the Goldstone Report never said or implied that the principal objective of Israel's attack was to murder Palestinians. If the Report did allege this, it would have had to charge Israel with genocide—but it didn't.

ONE MIGHT WONDER why the Goldstone Report should have triggered so much vituperation in Israel and set off a global diplomatic blitz to contain the fallout from it. After all, the Goldstone Mission's findings were merely the last in a long series of human rights reports condemning Israeli actions in Gaza, and Israel has never been known for its deference to U.N. bodies.

The answer however is not hard to find. Goldstone is not only Jewish but—in his own words—a "Zionist" who "worked for Israel all of my adult life," "fully support[s] Israel's right to exist" and is a "firm believer in the absolute right of the Jewish people to have their home there."

Goldstone has also claimed the Nazi holocaust as the seminal inspiration for the international law and human rights agenda of which he is a leading exponent. Because of Goldstone's credentials, Israel could not credibly play its usual cards—"anti-Semite," "self-hating Jew," "Holocaust denier"—against him.

In effect Goldstone's persona neutralized the ideological weapons Israel had honed over many years to ward off criticism.

Compelled to face the facts and their consequences, disarmed and exposed, Israel went into panic mode. Influential Israeli columnists expressed alarm that the Goldstone Report might impede Israel's ability to launch military attacks in the future. Prime Minister Netanyahu ranked "the Iranian [nuclear] threat, the missile threat and a threat I call the Goldstone threat" the major strategic challenges confronting Israel.

In the meantime Israeli officials fretted that prosecutors might pursue Israelis traveling abroad. And indeed, shortly after the Goldstone Report was published, the International Criminal Court announced it was contemplating an investigation of an Israeli officer implicated in the Gaza invasion. In December 2009 Tzipi Livni cancelled a trip to London after a British court issued an arrest warrant for her role in the commission of war crimes while serving as foreign minister and member of the war cabinet during the invasion.

"Months after it was published," an Israeli columnist rued, "the Goldstone Report still holds the top spot in the bestseller list of Israel's headaches."

On 1 April 2011 Israel's headache went away.

GOLDSTONE JUSTIFIES his recantation in the *Washington Post* on the grounds that "we know a lot more today about what happened" during the Israeli invasion than when the Mission compiled the Report. On the basis of this alleged new information he suggests that Israel did not commit war crimes in Gaza and that Israel is fully capable on its own of investigating any violations of international law that did occur.

It is correct that much new information on what happened during the Israeli invasion has become available since publication of the Mission's Report. But the vast preponderance of this new material sustains and even extends the Report's findings.

In addition to those already cited in the Goldstone Report, many more Israeli combatants stepped forward in 2010 to confirm egregious aspects of the Israeli invasion.

For example, an officer who served at a brigade headquarters recalled that IDF policy amounted to ensuring "literally zero risk to the soldiers," while a combatant remembered a meeting with his brigade commander and others where it was conveyed that "if you see any signs of movement at all you shoot. This is essentially the rules of engagement."

Goldstone could have cited this new information to buttress the Mission's Report but chose to ignore it.

In 2010 Human Rights Watch published a report based on satellite imagery documenting numerous cases "in which Israeli forces caused extensive destruction of homes, factories, farms and greenhouses in areas under IDF control without any evident military purpose. These cases occurred when there was no fighting in these areas; in many cases, the destruction was carried out during the final days of the campaign when an Israeli withdrawal was imminent."

Goldstone could have cited this new information to buttress the Mission's Report but again chose to ignore it.

How is it possible to take seriously Goldstone's claim that the facts compelled him to recant when he scrupulously ignores the copious new evidence confirming the Mission's Report?

SINCE PUBLICATION of the Goldstone Report Israel has released many purported refutations of it. The most voluminous of these was a 350-page report compiled by the Israeli Intelligence and Terrorism Information Center in 2010, *Hamas and the Terrorist Threat from the Gaza Strip: The main findings of the Goldstone Report versus the factual findings*.

The Israeli document was based on unverifiable "reports from IDF forces" and "Israeli intelligence information," indecipherable photographic evidence and information gathered from "terrorist operatives" who had been tortured.

It falsely alleged that the Goldstone Report made "almost no mention of the brutal means of repression used by Hamas against its opponents"; that the Report devoted "just three paragraphs" to Hamas's "rocket and mortar fire" during the Israeli invasion; that the Report "absolved" Hamas "of all responsibility for war crimes"; that the Report gave "superficial" treatment to "the terrorist organizations' use of civilians as human shields"; and that the Report depended on "the unreliable casualty statistics provided by Hamas."

It is hard to reconcile the mendacity of Israel's most ambitious attempt to refute the Goldstone Report with Goldstone's claim that new Israeli information fatally undermines the Mission's findings.

THE HEART of Goldstone's recantation is that on the basis of new information he has concluded that "civilians were not intentionally targeted as a matter of policy." It is not entirely clear what is being asserted here.

If Goldstone is saying that he no longer believes Israel had a *systematic policy* of targeting Gaza's civilian population *for murder*, his recantation is gratuitous because the Mission's Report never made such a claim. If the Report had made such a claim it would have verged on charging Israel with genocide. But the Report never even came close to entertaining, let alone leveling, such a charge.

What the Goldstone Report did say was that Israel's invasion of Gaza was a "deliberately disproportionate attack designed to punish, humiliate and terrorize a civilian population."

In fact the Goldstone Report assembles compelling evidence that as a matter of policy Israel resorted to indiscriminate, disproportionate force against the civilian population of Gaza. Goldstone does not allege in his *Washington Post* op-ed that new information calls this evidence into doubt.

Israeli leaders themselves did not shy away from acknowledging the indiscriminate, disproportionate nature of the attack they launched.

As the invasion wound down Foreign Minister Tzipi Livni declared that it had "restored Israel's deterrence . . . Hamas now understands that when you fire on [Israel's] citizens it responds by going wild—and this is a good thing." The day after the ceasefire Livni bragged on Israeli television that "Israel demonstrated real hooliganism during the course of the recent operation, which I demanded."

A former Israeli defense official told the International Crisis Group that "with an armada of fighter planes attacking Gaza, Israel decided to play the role of a mad dog for the sake of future deterrence," while a former senior Israeli security official boasted to the Crisis Group that Israel had regained its deterrence because it "has shown Hamas, Iran and the region that it can be as lunatic as any of them."

"The Goldstone Report, which claimed that Israel goes crazy when it is being attacked, caused us some damage," a leading Israeli commentator on Arab affairs observed, "yet it was a blessing in our region. If Israel goes crazy and destroys everything in its way when it is being attacked, one should be careful. No need to mess with crazy people."

It is an integral principle of law that "the doer of an act must be taken to have *intended* its natural and foreseeable consequences" (Judge Christopher Weeramantry, International Court of Justice). Thus, an indiscriminate, disproportionate attack that inevitably and predictably results in civilian deaths is indistinguishable from a deliberate and intentional attack on civilians.

"There is no genuine difference between a premeditated attack against civilians (or civilian objects) and a reckless disregard of the principle of distinction" between civilians (or civilian objects) and combatants (or military objects), according to Israel's leading authority on international law, Yoram Dinstein—"they are equally forbidden."

If Goldstone now believes that because Israel did not intentionally target civilians for murder it is not guilty of war crimes, he ought to brush up on the law: an indiscriminate, disproportionate attack on civilian areas is no less criminal.

If he now believes that it is not criminal behavior for an invading army to go "wild," demonstrate "real hooliganism," carry on like a "mad dog," act "lunatic" and "crazy," and "destroy everything in its way," then he should not be practicing law.

TO SUSTAIN his implied contention that Israel did not commit *any* war crimes because it *never* targeted civilians, Goldstone cites the notorious case of the al-Samouni family. Below I juxtapose his account of what a new Israeli investigation allegedly shows beside (1) the account he gave at a Stanford University forum two months prior to his recantation, (2) the account of Amnesty International in March 2011, and (3) the account of a March 2011 U.N. report that he praises. I have put in bold face what Goldstone omits:

Goldstone op-ed	Goldstone (Stanford)
[T]he most serious attack the Goldstone Report focused on was the killing of some 29 members of the al-Simouni [sic] family in their home. The shelling of the home was apparently the consequence of an Israeli commander's erroneous interpretation of a drone image.	[T]he single most serious incident reported in the [Goldstone] Report—[was] the bombing of the home of the al-Samouni family. ... On January 4, 2009, members of the Givati Brigade of **the IDF decided to take over the house of Saleh al-Samouni as part of the IDF ground operation; they ordered its occupants to relocate to the home of Wa'el al-Samouni. It was located about 35 yards away and within sight of the Israeli soldiers.** ... In the result there were over 100 members of the family gathered in the single story home of Wa'el al-Samouni. **Early on the cold wintry morning of 5 January, several male members of the al-Samouni family went outside to gather firewood. They were in clear sight of the Israeli troops.** As the men returned with the firewood, projectiles fired from helicopter gunships killed or injured them. Immediately after that further projectiles hit the house. Twenty-one members of the family were killed, some of them young children and women. Nineteen were injured. Of those injured, another eight subsequently died from their injuries. ... [This evidence] led the Fact-Finding Mission to conclude that, as a probability, the attack on the al-Samouni family constituted a deliberate attack on civilians. The crucial consideration was that **the men, women and children were known by the Israeli troops to be civilians and were ordered by them to relocate to a house that was**

in the vicinity of their command post. Members of the al-Samouni family had regarded the presence of the IDF as a guarantee of their safety.

...

[A]t the end of October 2010 (almost 22 months after the incident), to the credit of the **Israeli Military Police, they announced that they were investigating whether the air strike against the al-Samouni home was authorized by a senior Givati brigade commander who had been warned of the danger to civilians.**

At about the same time there were reports that the attack followed upon the receipt of photographs by the Israeli military from a drone showing what was incorrectly interpreted to be a group of men carrying rocket launchers towards a house. The order was given to bomb the men and the building. According to these reports, the photograph received from the drone was not of high quality and in fact showed the men carrying firewood to the al-Samouni home. The results of this military police investigation are as yet unknown.

Amnesty International	U.N. committee report
One prominent case that was examined by the [Goldstone Mission] and various human rights groups and is the subject of an ongoing Israeli criminal investigation is the killing of some 21 members of the al-Sammouni family, who were sheltering in the home of Wa'el al-Sammouni when it was struck by missiles or shells on 5 January 2009. The Israeli military announced that an MPCID [Military Police Criminal Investigations Division] investigation had been opened into this incident on 6 July 2010. On 21 October 2010, Colonel Ilan Malka, who was commander of the Givati Brigade . . . and was allegedly involved in approving the air strike which killed 21 members of the al-Sammouni family, was questioned under caution by military police. According to media reports, he claimed that he was unaware of the presence of civilians in the building when he approved the strike. The decision to approve the air strike was reportedly based on drone photographs of men from the al-Sammouni family breaking apart boards for firewood; the photographs were interpreted in the war room as Palestinians armed with	The Committee does not have sufficient information to establish the current status of the ongoing criminal investigations into the killings of Ateya and Ahmad Samouni, the attack on the Wa'el al-Samouni house and the shooting of Iyad Samouni. This is of considerable concern: reportedly 24 civilians were killed and 19 were injured in the related incidents on 4 and 5 January 2009. Furthermore, the events may relate both to the actions and decisions of soldiers on the ground and of senior officers located in a war room, as well as to broader issues implicating the rules of engagement and the use of drones. . . . Media reports further inform that a senior officer, who was questioned "under caution" and had his promotion put on hold, told investigators that he was not warned that civilians were at the location. **However, some of those civilians had been ordered there by IDF soldiers from that same officer's unit and air force officers reportedly informed him of the possible presence of civilians. Despite allegedly being made aware of this information, the officer apparently approved air strikes that killed 21 people**

GOLDSTONE RECANTS   25

Amnesty International	U.N. committee report
rocket-propelled grenades. But at the time the photographs were received, the family had already been confined to the building and surrounded and observed by soldiers from the Givati Brigade in at least six different nearby outposts for more than 24 hours; at least some soldiers in these outposts would have known that the family were civilians since they themselves had ordered the family to gather in Wa'el al-Sammouni's home. Some of these officers reportedly testified to the military investigators that they had warned Colonel Malka that there could be civilians in the area. [endnotes omitted]	and injured 19 gathered in the al-Samouni house. Media sources also report that the incident has been described as a legitimate interpretation of drone photographs portrayed on a screen and that the special command investigation, initiated ten months after the incidents, did not conclude that there had been anything out of the ordinary in the strike. . . . The same officer who assertedly called in the strike reportedly insisted that ambulances not enter the sector under his control, fearing attempts to kidnap soldiers. [endnotes omitted]

Goldstone has excised all the evidence casting doubt on the new Israeli alibi. His depiction of the facts in his recantation might be appropriate if he were Israel's defense attorney but it hardly befits the head of a Mission that was mandated to ferret out the truth.

GOLDSTONE JUSTIFIES his recantation on the grounds that "we know a lot more today." It is unclear however what, if anything, "a lot more" consists of. He points to the findings of Israeli military investigations.

But what do "we know . . . today" about these in camera hearings except what Israel says about them? In fact Israel has furnished virtually no information on which to independently assess the evidence adduced or the fairness of these proceedings. It is not even known how many investigations are complete and how many still ongoing.

Although he claims to "know a lot more," and bases his recantation on this "a lot more," neither Goldstone nor anyone else could have independently assessed any of this purportedly new information before he recanted.

Even in the three investigations that resulted in criminal indictments, the proceedings were often inaccessible to the public (apart from the indicted soldiers' supporters) and full transcripts of the proceedings were not made publicly available. And surely no information that came out of these criminal indictments—one soldier was convicted of stealing a credit card and two others were convicted of using a Palestinian child as a human shield—could have caused Goldstone to *reverse* himself.

The key example of revelatory new information Goldstone cites is the alleged misreading of a drone image which caused Israel to mistakenly target an extended family of civilians. If, as humanitarian and human rights organizations declared right after the al-Samouni killings, it was one of the "gravest" and "most shocking" incidents of the Israeli assault, and if, as Goldstone said, the al-Samouni killings were "the single most serious incident" in the Mission's Report, it is odd that Israel did not rush to restore its bruised reputation after the Gaza invasion but instead waited 22 *months* before coming forth with such a simple explanation.

To defend Israel against the Mission's findings, the report *Hamas and the Terrorist Threat from the Gaza Strip* reproduced numerous Israeli aerial photographs taken during the Gaza assault. Why has Israel still not made publicly available this drone image that allegedly exonerates it of criminal culpability for the most egregious incident of which it was accused?

It is also cause for wonder why Goldstone credits this new Israeli "evidence" sight unseen, yet ignores genuinely new evidence revealed by Amira Hass in *Haaretz* after his Report's publication: that before the attack—the civilian deaths of which allegedly surprised the Givati brigade commander who ordered it—"a Givati force set up outposts and bases in at least six houses in the Samouni compound."

Didn't the Givati commander check with these soldiers on the ground before launching the murderous attack to make sure they were out of harm's way? Didn't he ask them whether they saw men carrying rocket launchers and didn't they reply no?

Israel might be able to furnish plausible answers in its defense. But Goldstone does not even bother to pose these obvious questions because "we know . . . today"—Israel said so—it was just a simple mistake.

After publication of the Mission's findings Israel had a ready, evidence-free explanation not just for the al-Samouni killings but also for many other war crimes documented in the Report. It alleged that the al-Bader flour mill was destroyed "in order to neutralize immediate threats to IDF forces"; that the Sawafeary chicken farm had been destroyed "for reasons of military necessity"; and that the al-Maqadmah mosque was targeted because "two terrorist operatives [were] standing near the entrance."

Do "we know . . . today" that the evidence of war crimes assembled in the Goldstone Report and thousands of pages of other human rights reports was all wrong just because Israel says so?

Did we also "know" that Israel didn't use white phosphorus during the Gaza assault because it repeatedly denied doing so?

THE ONLY other scrap of new information Goldstone references in his recantation is the recent figure supplied by a Hamas official of the number of Hamas combatants killed during the invasion that "turned out to be similar" to the official Israeli figure. This Hamas figure appeared to confirm Israel's claim that the majority of Gazans killed during the invasion were combatants, not civilians. But then Goldstone notes parenthetically that Hamas "may have reason to inflate" its figure. So why does he credit it?

To prove that it defeated Israel on the battlefield Hamas originally alleged that only 48 of its fighters had been killed. After the full breadth of Israel's destruction became apparent and the claims of a battlefield victory rang hollow, and in the face of accusations that the people of Gaza had paid the price of its reckless decisions, Hamas abruptly upped the figure by several hundred to show that it too had suffered major losses.

As Goldstone himself put it at Stanford just two months before his recantation, the new Hamas figure "was intended to bolster the reputation of Hamas with the people of Gaza."

Whereas Goldstone now defers to this politically inflated Hamas figure, the Mission's Report relied on numbers furnished by respected Israeli and Palestinian human rights organizations, each of which independently and meticulously investigated the aggregate and civilian/combatant breakdown of those killed.

Disputing Israel's claim that only 300 Gazan civilians were killed, these human rights organizations put the figure at some 800-1,200 and also demonstrated that Israeli figures lacked credibility.

Even the largely apologetic U.S. Department of State *2009 Human Rights Report* put the number of dead "at close to 1,400 Palestinians, including more than 1,000 civilians."

But because a politically manipulated Israeli figure chimes with a politically manipulated Hamas figure, Goldstone discards the much larger figure for Palestinian civilian deaths documented by human rights organizations and even validated by the U.S. State Department.

IN HIS RECANTATION Goldstone says he is "confident" that Israeli military investigations will bring those guilty of wrongdoing to justice and goes on to assert that Israel has already "done this to a significant degree." In fact in this instance we do have new data since publication of the Mission's findings but, alas, they hardly buttress Goldstone's newfound faith.

In the course of Israel's assault on Gaza, it damaged or destroyed "everything in its way," including 280 schools and kindergartens, 1,500 factories and workshops, electrical, water and sewage installations, 190 greenhouse complexes, 80 percent of agricultural crops, and nearly one-fifth of cultivated land.

Entire neighborhoods in Gaza were laid waste and some 600,000 tons of rubble were left behind after Israel withdrew.

More than two years after the Gaza invasion the only penalty Israel has imposed for unlawful property destruction was an unknown disciplinary measure taken against one soldier.

But Goldstone is now "confident" that Israeli wrongdoers will be punished and also asserts that Israel has already "done this to a significant degree."

Beyond killing 1,400 Palestinians (including more than 300 children) and the massive destruction it inflicted on civilian infrastructure, Israel damaged or destroyed 29 ambulances, almost half of Gaza's 122 health facilities (including 15 hospitals), and 45 mosques. It also—in the words of Human Rights Watch—"repeatedly exploded white phosphorus munitions in the air over populated areas, killing and injuring civilians, and damaging civilian structures, including a school, a market, a humanitarian aid warehouse and a hospital."

Both the Goldstone Report and human rights organizations concluded that much of this death and destruction would constitute war crimes.

More than two years after the Gaza invasion the only Israeli soldier who did jail time for criminal conduct served seven months after being convicted of credit card theft.

But Goldstone is now "confident" that Israeli wrongdoers will be punished and also asserts that Israel has already "done this to a significant degree."

To be sure Israel did express remorse at what happened in Gaza. "I am ashamed of the soldier," Information Minister Yuli Edelstein declared, "who stole some credit cards."

After this wondrous show of contrition how could Goldstone not be "confident" of Israel's resolve to punish wrongdoers?

IN HIS RECANTATION Goldstone can barely contain his loathing and contempt for Hamas. He says that—unlike in Israel's case—Hamas's criminal intent "goes without saying—its rockets were purposefully and indiscriminately aimed at civilian targets." The Mission's Report had reached this conclusion on the basis of a couple of statements by Hamas leaders combined with Hamas's actual targeting of these civilian areas.

It is unclear however why comparable statements by Israeli officials combined with Israel's purposeful and indiscriminate targeting of civilian areas in Gaza no longer prove Israel's criminal guilt. In fact judging by the Mission's findings, none of which Goldstone recants, the case against Israel was incontrovertible.

If, as Israel asserted and investigators found, it possessed fine "grid maps" of Gaza and an "intelligence gathering capacity" that "remained extremely effective"; and if it made extensive use of state-of-the-art precision weaponry; and if 99 percent of the firing that was carried out by the Air Force hit targets accurately; and if it only once targeted a building erroneously: then, as the Mission's Report logically concluded, the massive destruction Israel inflicted on Gaza's civilian infrastructure must have "resulted from deliberate planning and policy decisions throughout the chain of command, down to the standard operating procedures and instructions given to the troops on the ground."

Goldstone also chastises Hamas because—unlike Israel—it has "done nothing" to investigate the criminal conduct of Gazans during the Israeli invasion.

Hamas attacks killed three Israeli civilians and nearly destroyed one civilian home. The Israeli assault on Gaza killed as many as 1,200 civilians and nearly or totally destroyed more than 6,000 civilian homes. Hamas did not sentence anyone to prison for criminal misconduct whereas Israel sentenced one soldier to seven months prison time for stealing a credit card.

Isn't it blazingly obvious how much eviler Hamas is?

In his recantation Goldstone avows that his goal is to apply evenhandedly the laws of war to state and non-state actors. It is unlikely however that this admirable objective will be advanced by his double standards.

Goldstone now rues his "unrealistic" hope that Hamas would have investigated itself, while his detractors heap ridicule on his past naiveté. How could a terrorist organization like Hamas have possibly investigated itself? Only civilized countries like Israel are capable of such self-scrutiny. Indeed Israel's judicial record is indisputable testimony to this capacity.

The Israeli human rights organization Yesh Din found that, although thousands of Palestinian civilians were killed during the second intifada, only five Israeli soldiers were held criminally liable and not a single Israeli soldier was convicted on a murder or manslaughter charge, and that 80 percent of the investigations of violent assault by Israeli settlers against Palestinians in 2005 were closed without criminal indictments.

The Israeli human rights organization B'Tselem found that in the decade following the outbreak of the first intifada 1,300 Palestinians had been killed yet only 19 Israeli soldiers were convicted of homicide, and that for the period 2006-9 "a soldier who kills a Palestinian not taking part in hostilities is almost never brought to justice for his act."

IT IS CLEAR that Goldstone did not publish his recantation because "we know a lot more today." What Goldstone calls new information consists *entirely* of unverifiable assertions by parties with vested interests. The fact that Goldstone cannot cite any genuinely new evidence to justify his recantation is the most telling proof that none exists.

What then happened?

As already noted, ever since publication of the Mission's Report, Goldstone has been the object of a relentless smear campaign. Harvard professor Alan Dershowitz compared him to Auschwitz "Angel of Death" Josef Mengele, while the Israeli ambassador to the United States castigated his Report as even worse than "Ahmadinejad and the Holocaust deniers."

Goldstone was not the only one who came under attack. The U.N. Human Rights Council appointed the eminent international jurist Christian Tomuschat to chair a follow-up committee mandated to determine whether Israeli and Hamas officials were investigating the allegations in the Goldstone Report. Deciding that Tomuschat was insufficiently pliant, the Israel lobby hounded and defamed him until he had no choice but to step down.

Many aspects of Goldstone's recantation are perplexing.

Goldstone has the reputation of being very ambitious. Although he was savaged after publication of the Report, the tide began to turn in his favor this past year.

In Israel the newspaper *Haaretz* editorialized that it was "time to thank the critics for forcing the IDF to examine itself and amend its procedures. Even if not all of Richard Goldstone's 32 charges were solid and valid, some of them certainly were." In the United States, *Tikkun* magazine honored Goldstone at a gala 25th anniversary celebration. In South

Africa distinguished personalities such as Judge Dennis Davis, formerly of the Jewish Board of Deputies, publicly denounced a visit by Alan Dershowitz because, among other things, he had "grossly misrepresented the judicial record of Judge Richard Goldstone."

It is puzzling why an ambitious jurist at the peak of a long and distinguished career would commit what might be professional suicide, alienating his colleagues and throwing doubt on his judgment, when the tide of public opinion was turning in his favor.

Throughout his professional career Goldstone has functioned in bureaucracies and has no doubt internalized their norms. Yet, in a shocking rupture with bureaucratic protocol he dropped his bombshell without first notifying his colleagues on the Mission or anyone at the United Nations.

It is as if Goldstone feared confronting them beforehand because he knew that he didn't have grounds to issue a recantation and could not possibly defend it.

His worries proved well founded. Shortly after publication of his recantation Goldstone's three colleagues on the Mission—Christine Chinkin, Hina Jilani and Desmond Travers—issued a joint statement unequivocally affirming the Report's original findings: "We concur in our view that there is no justification for any demand or expectation for reconsideration of the report as nothing of substance has appeared that would in any way change the context, findings or conclusions of that report."

In his op-ed Goldstone alleges that it was new information on the killings of the al-Samouni family and the total number of Hamas combatants killed during the invasion that induced him to recant. But just two months earlier at Stanford University he matter-of-factly addressed these very same points without drawing any dramatic conclusions. No new evidence surfaced in the interim.

In his recantation Goldstone also references a U.N. document to give Israel a clean bill of health on its investigations although, as widely noted, this document was much more critical of Israeli investigations than he lets on.

It is as if Goldstone were desperately clutching at any shred of evidence, however problematic, to justify his recantation. Indeed he rushed to acquit Israel of criminal culpability in the al-Samouni deaths even before the Israeli military had completed its investigation.

A few days before submitting his op-ed to the *Washington Post*, Goldstone submitted another version of it to the *New York Times*. The *Times* rejected the submission apparently because it did not repudiate the Goldstone Report.

The impression one gets is of Goldstone being pressured against his will to publish a repudiation of the Report. To protect his reputation and because his heart is not in it, Goldstone submits a wishy-washy recantation to the *Times*. After the *Times* rejects it, and in a race against the clock, he hurriedly slips in wording that can be construed as a full-blown repudiation to make sure that the *Post* will run what is now a bombshell.

The exertion of outside pressure on Goldstone would perhaps also explain the murkiness of his op-ed, in which he seems to be simultaneously recanting and not recanting the Report, and his embarrassing inclusion of irrelevances such as a call on the Human Rights Council to condemn the slaughter of an Israeli settler family—two years after the Gaza invasion in an incident unrelated to the Gaza Strip—by unknown perpetrators.

THE EMINENT South African jurist John Dugard is a colleague of Goldstone's. Dugard also headed a fact-finding mission that investigated what happened in Gaza. The conclusions of his report—which contained a finer legal analysis while Goldstone's was broader in scope—largely overlapped with those of the Goldstone Mission: "the purpose of Israel's action was to punish the people of Gaza" and Israel was "responsible for the commission of internationally wrongful acts by reason of the commission of war crimes and crimes against humanity."

In a devastating dissection of Goldstone's recantation in the *New Statesman*, Dugard concluded: "There are no new facts that exonerate Israel and that could possibly have led Goldstone to change his mind. What made him change his mind therefore remains a closely guarded secret."

Although Goldstone's secret will perhaps never be revealed and his recantation has caused irreparable damage, it is still possible by patient reconstruction of the factual record to know the truth about what happened in Gaza. Out of respect for the memory of those who perished during the Gaza massacre we must preserve and protect this truth from its assassins.

Available exclusively at www.orbooks.com

"[Finkelstein's] place in the whole history of writing history is assured."
—Raul Hilberg, author, *The Destruction of the European Jews*

For the Palestinians who live in the narrow coastal strip of Gaza, the Israeli invasion of December 2008 was a nightmare of unimaginable proportions: In the 22-day-long action 1,400 Gazans were killed, several hundred on the first day alone.

And yet, while nothing should diminish Palestinian suffering through those frightful days, it is possible something redemptive is emerging from the tragedy of Gaza. For, as Norman Finkelstein details, in a concise work that melds cold anger with cool analysis, the profound injustice of the Israeli assault was widely recognized by bodies that it is impossible to brand as partial or extremist.

Amnesty International, Human Rights Watch, and the UN investigation headed by Richard Goldstone, in documenting Israel's use of indiscriminate and intentional force against the civilian population during the invasion (100 Palestinians died for every one Israeli), have had an impact on longstanding support for Israel. Jews in both the Unites States and the United Kingdom, for instance, have begun to voice dissent, and this trend is especially apparent among the young. Such a shift, Finkelstein contends, can create new pressure capable of moving the Middle East crisis towards a solution, one that embraces justice for Palestinians and Israelis alike.

This new paperback edition has been revised throughout and includes an extensive aft erword on the Israeli att ack on the Gaza Freedom Flotilla which resulted in the deaths of nine activists and further strained the loyalty of many of Israel's traditional allies around the world. It also contains a brand new appendix in which Finkelstein dissects the official Israeli investigation of the flotilla attack.

"A very impressive, learned and careful scholar."
—Avi Shlaim, Professor, International Relations, Oxford University

'THIS TIME WE WENT TOO FAR'
TRUTH AND CONSEQUENCES OF THE GAZA INVASION
Norman G. Finkelstein

Now in an expanded and revised paperback
Publication May 5 2011 7 1/2 x 8 1/4 inches
343 pages
Paperback ISBN 978-1-935928-43-0
E-book ISBN 978-1-935928-44-7